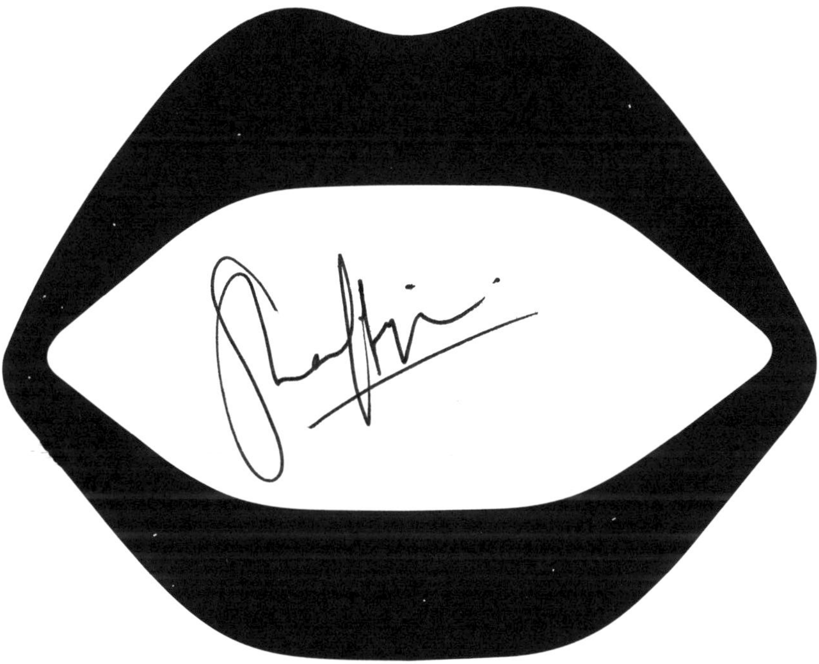

First published in 2024 by Rough Trade Books

First Edition

ISBN 978-1-914236-40-2

Design by Eliza Hart and Craig Oldham
at Office Of Craig

Bloemen in een vaas (Flowers in a Vase)
Jan Brueghel the Elder (1568–1625)

Printed in England

roughtradebooks.com

Open Mouths

Sharan Hunjan

ROUGH TRADE BOOKS

"There is no more sombre enemy of good art than the pram in the hall."

—Cyril Connolly

Contents

IV. SKY IS A MOUTH

V. BREATH

VI. O

O. TONGUE

Teach Like A—

Once, I shouted at a kid &   it wasn't his fault.

Thank you X . Thank you Y.   Track me.   Track the board.

I have 80%.   I have 90%   on target.

S c a n   the   r o o m

Be   Seen   Looking

A voice booms through the building:

White   male   identified.

Victim: Black male   *possibly* a juvenile.

Classroom in my lungs.   feels too full.

Green pens out.   Eyes.   On.   Me.

Is this the language   of warmth & safety.   A duty of care-

ful planning.   Tracking.   Hand signals.   *hold up**

*5 fingers**   *4 fingers**   *3 fingers**   *2 fingers**   *1 finger**   & shoot.

A removal   should be swift.   We take fingerprints

for lunch.   Registers check   who is M.I.A.

Thank you X. Thank you Y.   Track me.   Track the board.   Eyes on me.

Is this the language of war-   mth & safety.

Cold calling   is used to adapt police—   *I mean to write polite*—questioning.

Use wait time   to reduce cognitive—   *load up your weapons.*

In the training video   Black children rise up   with the white woman's hand

in 7 seconds   & she trains them   to do it in 4 seconds.

We prepare   for the trenches.   Equip

with tools   & strategies.   We exercise

repeatedly   for any   situation.

Detention   centres are full of humans   fleeing war.

Isolation   is the consistent behaviour   of loneliness.

Parental meetings   prosecute in a court of law   white walls watch like a jury.

We judge the working class—   room atmosphere   are they working

hard enough.   Is there a thirst

for learning.   We target a subject   to increase engagement.

You are   dismissed   on the bell.

Lapels line up with armies of badges   on children   of war.

Once, I noticed all the sanctions   written on my board

were for children   who were Black.

You have 3 strikes   & then you're out.   This is the language of warnings. Deploy the SANCTION system. Foreign policy

for behaviour. *–Strike 1* Sanctity is lost.

–Strike 2 Sanctimonious behaviour is unacceptable.

–Strike 3

Reports are filed in prisons too.

–Target has been removed.

Pariah

Billy bosh I'm jammin' mate!

Bish bash bob's yer uncle!

Loot the store   I'm a damned juggernaut from the jungle
pinch punch   first day of the month—

I got a mouth full of pickle...   *a tongue full of chutney...*

—I'm an avatar baby   take those bangles
bangles of Blighty   smash them on your wedding day
in your khaki dungarees   *you'll get your kharma mate*
it'll bite you in the balls   smash you on the nose—
PUNCH!—

That's five ingredients

panj ingredients

to make your bowl of booze
& it'll all be tickety-boo   *sab teek hai babu*   that's tickety-boo
now fetch me a hot toddy in the midst of these typhoons!

Use shampoo   you look like a thug

repeat the mantra baby—
chit chat chit chat   we used to write chittis
letters & letters   send me a chitti from the pind
tell me life in the Raj is cushty   *it's pukka mate*

it's higgledy-piggledy topsy-turvy tit-for-tat hocus-pocus
take me transform me wind me up knock me
down turn me around   *I'm your plaything...*
end in your down-legged-dog pose   warrior pose

'cause I'm a pariah in my own bungalow
in my pyjamas eating basmati & daal
sitting in my yoga pose
with my chakras all aligned—

& when I'm out let's say Namaste

let's say Namaste

let's say Namaste

so cross your legs

bow your heads

smell your sweat

& repeat after me

NAM - AS - TEY

I .BEAST

Homerton Birthing Centre

I walk on holy water

I drop
to my knees pray in the name of Allah
I stop a rock imprint my hand in stone

a Guru hair uncut tied to a branch
silver beech eyes closed
hiss of a snake by my feet

For her I turn empty baskets into hot bread
& fish that shine moonlight
I press my forehead to the floor
pull apart an ocean

turn to face the nurse my face wet with salt still
I am the trumpet the tabla the vājā
words of prayer carried by storms
wake the villagers at dawn

I died I am resurrected
wrists nailed crown burning
sat on a fiery stove imprisoned Guru

I walk the earth spreading the word
I am every Granth Sahib Qur'an Bible
wash your hands before you touch me
scrape the dirt from your feet
hide your breath behind your hands
for her wail is the mourners' delight
the cry the sign that I came back to life

The Price We Pay

At the door we make the transaction.

They tell me, *she'll enjoy the company*
of other babies. Get socialised.
She protests at the door.
I tell them of her milk strike as her fists resist,
her cries a chant, a banner in the air
a placard of angry paint.
She strikes out. Revolts
as they pacify her with oohs & coos & plastic toys, my poor girl
her fat cheeks filled red, a labour of love.

She is anarchy, throwing stones & stinging tear gas.
I buy time by removing her fluffy coat   s l o w l y
holding her close. Hot skin on cold fingers.
I say, *remember Nafeesa?* We exchange smiles.
You like her glasses, her long dark hair, trying to sell this stranger to my baby.
(She's not buying it.)
After the handover we briefly trade pleasantries
thanks, lovely, great, bye then!
packaged, Sello-taped like a delivery.

I venture to work through the cold war
of icy wind, white concrete, wealth of cars.
Grey industrial trees stand rooted like individuals.
This is the price we pay
balancing our babies, bricks & bread.

When I collect her later, they tell me her welfare state.
The report: *she played with pots*
ate
cried when the other babies cried.

I pop my baby into her coat
her zip running down her throat
like a tie. When she looks up at me optimistically
my smile strains, cuts, calculating the austerity of love.

Wolf Mother

Wolf mother tunes the radio dial.
Wolf mother's ears prick up, sharp
like roofs of houses. Wolf mother's window eyes
watch carcasses of leaves, black bark of trees.
Wolf mother's shadow lies like a snare.
Wolf mother picks up paws, retreats
into waves of self. Wolf mother breathes firmness
of flesh & blood. Wolf mother sniffs at this hum
& reaches below the bed of flowing, knowing river.
Wolf mother interrogates earth's pull of magnetic core
hears it turn like cogs in a clock. Wolf mother weighs up moon
& predator. Wolf mother digs for the river word.
Wolf mother stalks under moonlight shining in streaks.
Wolf mother's word left curled
inside the closed palm of a full stop.

Silent Night

Because a fox screeches outside
& Waheguru is stuck in my throat.

Because worries of the day rack up like a receipt
which I pay for after dark. Because over toast

slippers & coffee I'll find the app on my phone,
tap 'Japji Sahib', pour milky teeth

into yolk. *Oh, holy morning!* Because He hung
like a leaf cross-legged. Because holy words

there are holes in my words—
in my worlds—because there are holes

in my worlds, because I wonder about you—holy—
because your words, your worlds, thrown

caught in palms press
close to my chest in prayer.

Because I repeat your name like a chant.
Because you sleep soundly

like a meditation
through the wide-eyed night.

mothers stuffed in pillowcases

hey just put it down
cover it up
shove your boob

back into your bra
your wild hair
is being pulled

by every suckle
move the strap
back to your shoulder

it isn't worth it
to lay yourself
on the ground

all doors & windows
locked down
so newborn mothers

are stuffed
into pillowcases
& babies bundles

of old sheets
no one to pull you
out of rubble

which broke
when you opened
 split   a   little   shifted

a little
in the two-bed flat
tight-lipped walls

rocked dark
of night
so only you

could smell
the fresh rain
of milk

II. FEAST

A Feast of Phrases

Air is spilt salt.
Sentences lie on the table like a knife
& fork. Tiny mouth, barely open
'o' dipped in yoghurt, thick, smears
bilabial consonants across her lips.
Alveolar sounds stick to her tongue & backs of teeth
swallowing, passing her velum, sinking
to a loud glottal stop.
Congealed stickiness on fingers are voiceless
her cup a short syllable
breath is dropped
milk that spreads thin.
Her plate round & continuous.
The table spreads as a continent
I sit on the left, you on the right
the tablecloth a spectrum
of love. Children & their open mouths
wait to be fed, wait for plates to be filled
hungry cries consume what we cook up,
bake, fry. Enzymes in her tummy churn
turn bolus around in their hands, make sense of,
disperse around her little arms & legs
sit inside her body, wedged like words you say
& can't take back. She picks up the spoon & feeds herself.

FEED

stories are worlds we finger

SCROLL UP

enter eyes, seep into skin

sit as a smile eating the camera

rain plays—is it air, wind or there

SCROLL MORE

thumb moves like a joystick

flowers fall from a vase, that is quiet

a picture is made of wood, opens & closes, is the threshold
to a room you don't want to enter

tomorrow/time/now is crumpled

SCROLL FURTHER

jealousy is bright electrical currents

CLICK

eyes burn

CLICK

feeding becomes a frenzy

a binge   we throw up inside ourselves

LIKE

what we don't

LIKE

is not a verb but a button

HEART

is a cold tap of options
a) I want this
b) I wish this was me
c) I hate you
d) other

SWIPE

monstrous feast full as buckets of KFC & grease of McDonalds

POST

is not an envelope sealed with a sender's lick of good intent

but a bill, a FINAL WARNING, sheets of paper, somebody's labour

POST

is no longer private, name & address scrawled on its back

crawls on hands & knees

PRO FILE

block of ice C.V. of life

a dull document

we swirl in nothing

COMMENTS

mute air filling our mouths

conversations in our heads like an illness

HOME

is a page we can't settle on

nowhere to sit

FEED

never ends like the deep of night when a beast is ravenous at your breast

Recipe

Let's make a baby.
Mix sugar, flour
salt of the earth, my eggs.
Shaped with our hands
kneaded by our bodies
bound by our kiss, our kiss
rising with fire.

Grenade

It's only after you text that I break
open the pomegranate
that's been sitting at the back of the fridge for weeks, stoically.
Its pink blood splatters all over the white work surface
as I dig. Excavating arils, crunch
of a searching spoon breaks beads
dotted like omniscient eyes,
cuts through crusts, uncovers caves
wrecking the place. It's messy & I wish I hadn't started.
Coming to an end, fevered hands plunge
deeper under tunnels discovering seeds cowering
like groups of hiding people. I scrape them out forcefully.
My fingers show up unannounced.
I chuck the hollow carcasses in the bin: two hard skins, a severed head (or heart).
Who would've thought the old fruit to have had so much blood in it.
Wiping away all splashes—fridge, toaster, floor—the knife
sits in a pool of red bloated in the sink.

Neighbours

We snipped pieces of A4 paper into shreds
for bowls of food. The gap between the bunk beds
was the café counter. Hardback books were plates.
We undid our long plaits

to be women. Lucious blow-dried hair
cascaded down tiny shoulders
as we served our stuffed animal customers
whilst dolls mimed as background extras.

We pushed back walls, pulled open the ceiling
to an Aussie blue-block God. Cameras rolling
we tied knots. T-shirts gathered at bellies.
We decided our roles. We assumed identities.

Susan enters the café. Toadfish orders milkshakes.
We smiled. Pleased the audience. We were fakes,
men, owners, teenagers, doctors, patients.
We re-enacted drama, fights, flirtations,

spat words from our mouths.
Teddies & dolls sat dumbfound
at the roles we played
at the people we became.

Scrambled Eggs

After an evening of trying to get you to eat chana & rice
saying *it's curry it's curry you eat it at nursery*
when I would *never* call it *curry*, it is just chana,

you wail at the thari I've blended for you.
Onions, tomatoes, ginger, garlic I've chopped.
Spices *(expensive-organic-shop-bought!)* simmered over heat.

I down white wine as you cry
eyes watching my eyes waiting for me to soothe.
I hold the side of the table to stop myself from falling.

I give you scrambled eggs & toast instead,
proper English café grub.
Happily, you stuff it behind the doors of your lips

decorate the floor as I pack away the pots & pans
throw away spices which melt with rain
disappearing through the gutter.

Nothing that goes in or comes out of your mouth
is what came out of my mother's
mother's mother's mouth.

I pick bits of egg off the floor
stuffing them behind my teeth, crowding up my stomach
scavenging for something that is not there.

C4 News

I order pessimism
with a side of tofu.

Korean rice, sticky television,
cheap corner shop wine.

Burnt voices. Take care
not to gauge my eyeballs out

with chopsticks. Glare
of humanity's

belly-filled
stained fingers.

Un-compostable
plastic night.

III. TEETH

Body of Water

Stomach is a fish floundering.
Mind a spinning reel.

My angling back
is bent like a rod

weighted down by a catch.
The swell of open sea

untethers my feet.
Ideas slip through fingers

like water.
I am drowning

in the chaos
of choppy waters

as waves lap
like her cries.

The Fall

A woman walks past me   asks *are you alright*
keeping a distance   my voice picks itself up off the wet ground   *I fell off my bike*
I don't say he jumped off the building
but you're ok though she asks   still walking   *yes* I say
but not ok   not ok   he said he was ok but we are not ok
she walks on   legs   intact
he fell   I fell   I get up   soothe
arm   wrist   pick up my bike   walk home   he stayed crumpled
I unlock the door
& there you are   when words fall from my mouth
like teeth   you hug me   I go to A&E to be saved by X-rays   to be saved
to burst into fresh tears when the nurse asks   *what happened?*
I don't mention the funeral but start with the fall   my fall
he tells me funny stories   people are nice   gives me a sling
I am able to get up   walk home   body   bones intact   crawl into bed   falling
into bed   no hard ground   but softness   cloud
crumpled in bed   day racing past   like cars   legs warm under covers
faces were wet today   ground was wet   racing home on my bike
day is tangled legs   I untangle
I fall   you fall   into sleep
like falling from a building   falling deep   into sleep

Phlegm

throat lurches towards lungs / claws a gooey handful / gunky & claggy between fingers / plugs the hole at the back of my mouth / like the past / it coagulates / makes a mess of now / disturbs conversation / disrupts / quiet / people turn & stare / as it bubbles up / blocks consonants / strangles diphthongs / spit it out again & again / interfering beast / pain in the night / darkens like thoughts / which spiral / restless 2 am / covers are moonlit / spit into a tissue / sink, empty coffee mug, whatever's nearby / congealed bronchioles / alveoli are blackened clouds / strained by polluted air / mix salt with hot water / a heady potion / therapist has gone on holiday for a month & this cough / flares / hijacks like a sick devil / or an old self that sticks / coughs itself up

Does Fire Ask Permission?

You sent me a poem
as a gift, wrapped in plastic, dirtied
by delivery men, by boxes
chucked place to place.

You said *I didn't mean it like that*
my pen ate my fingers & ran away
my pen posted it to everybody.

I shoved sorries down the phone
& the telephone wire
choked, sparked, caught a terrible fire,
a fire as big as London,

like a drunk man falling—
this isn't what *I* said
this is *the fire*—devouring buildings & roads
burning cafés & shops—black as ash & ink.

Fires never ask permission.
They mean to 'warm', 'give light'.
It was a mistaken fire. It was me. I did it.
I wrote about you.

Sister Rach

Sister Rach broke up with the Church. They deleted her
from the Youth WhatsApp Group. Later, they deleted her
from the Women's WhatsApp Group. The pastor 'dear Rachel'd'
her over text. *Six years,* she said, *six years old.*
Choir, Sundays, Bible study. Hours
so easily He hath taken away. Judas-eyed, they turned
their backs when she was on her knees. Her voice was a body
that danced in between the pews. They gorged
on wine & bread, asking if she was okay
with bloody lips. Mother & daughter ousted
by the flash of a diamond ring on a foreign finger.
She dismantled her voice. Silence sits deeper
into the cushioned seat of her being making itself at home.
Over eggs, she says she hasn't ovulated since.
A panic attack in the night is like a dream, you can pretend it didn't happen.
The waiter brings us water which we pour onto white chairs
& tables, a holy brunch blessing. At the till she says,
me & God are still like this, showing me a cross, a finger wrapping around the other.

IV. SKY IS A MOUTH

Heron

No fish, says the child.
Filthy water in detritus, in stink.

Tyres, flat & abandoned,
picture of a temple, sunk,
a white jug painted with soil,
cracking dry mud, burnt tortoise shell
bricks—so many bricks—thrown,
broken—this is the very bottom—broken—
this is the very bottom of the canal.

Ducks still dip their heads.

Channel chatter through pipes,
snapped canes, grooves of earth
changed, cut & criticised.
The hidden part
for all park goers to see,
to say, *how disgusting, how dirty,*
so that's what's underneath.

Perched is the heron—a distant owner—
its thin leg stuck like a pin.

Snow Leopard

Scoop with a tongue which curves like words:
uncia once l'unce lynx feliformia panther relic uncial
All its names roll onto its back. Thickly formed tail
of storage fat, furry as a blanket night over Himalayas.
Eyes fling open at dawn, moan while broad paws pad
out of bed, tail keeping balance, as it pours coffee.
Purrs at a whisper, no roar is waiting here, no
moving through the house lying in a throat
waiting to pounce. No roar—a solitary *meow.*
Nothing pacing around evenings. Solitary
fur coat. Elevated forehead. No roar around here.
Fierce upright blue, a spotted cat is losing
itself, we are losing, under mountains & a quiet crush of snow.
Canines folded, stored in the cupboard of its mouth.

Luna

Moonblind, I run weighing up the cruelty of being loved.
Exercise a de-centred core
from waves of waxing & waning.
Fully illuminated between sun & earth
suboptimal time for running shoes,
shadows amplified, contracted to move
my body. It is synodic, face to face.
I dreamt my eye watered like a tap,
pierced, I rubbed & rubbed.
Curled up, lunate, my insomnia turns itself away.
I rub my eye like a lunatic,
a mother, a maiden, a crone, dissolves
in morning pitch black lust.
My body surges, urging me to put on headphones
& run, a lycanthropic pull out of bed
towards the moon—touching distance.
Dream awake. Black oiled earth
is dipped in darkness.

There Are No Birds Down Here

heat turned up 200 degrees we are cooked meat in a hot oven / sweating men with guns
stomp down the platform / & when his gun whacks the pole
/ we jump /
bit by tiny bit you
bite your apple / held like a precious offering in two sticky palms / I read on my knees
pointing to each detail of the book / decorated voice / an old couple watches / floor of
the tube thick with grime / flowered skirt pretends it is spring / on the intercom the
driver had said stuck doors at London Bridge but I tell you I think he lied / there are
no birds down here / shooting through hot carriages bomb shelters commuter hell /
people offer me a seat but their eyes hope I will say no / armed police spit in walkie-
talkies searching for two men / *(I am afraid)* / this whole train will
/ blow /
legs kick chest strapped eyes search / there are / no / birds / watching / in the corner
/ down / here / nothing but rats & humans / deep / lifts & escalators run deep / you
point at the book / make bird sounds / deep / a bird would flutter / fall / deep / tunnels
flash through windows / dark rumbles & screeches / your eyes fill with bright fright /
I want to pluck you / pop you in a park / watch you run arms hands fluttering mouth
squawking hair bunches flying / in the blue sky infinite

Trying Not to Use a Bird Metaphor

Bird metaphors with all their wings, broken
beaks singing—I delete. Cut pigeons who strut
fat from the city's rubbish. Erase crow shadows
stalking beer-bottle-takeaway-box-filled bins.
Cross out parakeets ecstatic in treetops.

I type *Watch your fingers!* as you peck
at the chicken's cage. Laughing, *cluck*
clucking! Poking its tail, you shout   *BIRD!*
They shoot into the blue page
air startled by sweeping voice.

You squash ant words, thwack tails of letters
paw a donkey, chat to dogs, *hiya doggy!*
Fly into the poem with hair soft as feathers
little chick curling into my lap before eggs crack,
yolk spills, doors fling wide open.

Arrival

Storm Eunice blasts our quiet days
of tea, getting dressed for work, making the bed.
We shut ourselves up inside, take plant pots off walls
shelter behind brick. We charge our phones, bottle up water,
stock the fridge with milk & bread. Put a wash on.

Air cramps, breaths start slow, getting faster
& faster as outside hedges thrash.
Debris flies in the throat of the sky, a whirlwind
maps around us, tables & chairs gasp, our hands grip nothing.
Birds are takeaway boxes flapping wildly mid-air.

Car alarms blare, air a thick ringing
water bursts through swollen clouds.
This force shuts down the city's shops & parks.
Reports of a giant oak, roots ripping
smack onto a Mercedes—metal cracks, windows shatter.

We stroll the aftermath: branches sticks twigs twisted
puddles lie on the ground of our minds.
Leaves are soggy skin on kerbs. Mud a squelching
clean trainers stick to. Plastic tape rattles around a circle of trees
who, like nurses, watch a breathless eucalyptus on its knees.

Moths

The moths creep along our white walls, the bastards.
First one or two, then a battle of them. Squash them
hoover them up, smack them as they flit past my face
invade this space. They attack, I attack.
I wonder if this one is Him

innocently creeping above my headboard.
As I read my book He orbits the sun-like lamp.
With a silent growl I squash it with a tissue, smear
a brown mark on my white wall & it is done.
Did I just fail the test?

I chuck Him in the bin, whoever it is.
Walls, specked with brown blood, have witnessed my sin.
I fall asleep with them feasting on my curtains
my clothes, the dark.

The Only Time Borderless is Okay

Meet your new ***Borderless Currency Card!*** *Empowers each employee! Cheaper transaction fees at home or abroad! Spend globally in multiple currencies without the cost!*

V. BREATH

18 Months Later

When things fall apart you buy kiwis, thumb their coarse softness
get packets of spinach, almonds, forget things.
At the checkout you plead

to go back, search aisles
for breath you left
near the biscuits.

When things fall apart you start to cook—
see stubs where your
hands used to be.

When things fall apart you hold your feet, swollen
traffic-light red, in fingers—*yes*, you still
have fingers.

When things fall apart you collect your body parts
—fingernails, elbows, thighs, stomach, legs—
hold them up in arms—apologise

for arriving too late. Flick a fly from eyes
look up to blank sky like a child
asking for something to eat.

When things fall apart you forget to ask
how are
you.

When things fall apart it's like
an army of ants building
a silent city.

When things fall apart you remember you have skin
when sun pushes clouds apart
sheds itself on you.

When things fall apart you wake up & realise you fell
asleep under midday sun & it lied–
it burned you anyway.

When things fall apart you don't want to kiss
or hear your baby's
laugh.

When things fall, a
part of you
runs.

Hatch

I just heard your heartbeat and it bounced around the room. Up

down

left right.

The midwife let it play,

a song

a hum

a dance.

Hatch II

It's a dirty kitchen
crumbs on the coffee table,
an un-hoovered, dirty floor,
stains on the bathroom mirror
where I avoid looking at myself
in the eye. It's the hum
of the fridge in the silence
when she's finally asleep
and *you just don't know how long it'll last.*
It's wanting to breathe
an anxious walk in the park
fresh air cutting your skin
hoping it'll make you feel alive again.
It's the wailing baby at midnight
and knowing. This. Is. It.
It's seeing someone fly by on their bike
through the crack in the blinds
when you're rocking her to sleep
strained 6 am wrists.
And it's not ending (the poem) with 'her sweet smile
that makes it all worthwhile'
or the wonder or awe or miracle
but it's the feeling of never-ending
it's the hesitant, desperate call
for someone to listen,
not to the cries, but to the silence.

Found-Ling Poem

Archive footage from The Foundling Museum / The Essential First Year: What babies need parents to know by Penelope Leach

Even a cuddle would've been nice, even a pat on the head.
It's time for the three of you to meet face to face and skin to skin.

But you didn't get it.
Many mothers' first reaction to their babies is kept so low-key by exhaustion, or feelings of relief at the birth being over, that bonding doesn't seem to come into it.

Tongue tied up for talking too much.
In the past it was thought that unless the anchoring skin was cut, the baby would not be able to suck properly or be able to talk.

Grace.
Distraction doesn't help babies eat.

You were not allowed to speak during the course of the meal
Baby-led or parent-led weaning?

Awful, awful white margarine.
Don't ever (now or next year) try to force food in her mouth when she is rejecting it, or keep pursuing her with the spoon when she's trying to avoid it by turning her head away.

I look back and I think, how cruel, how could you do that?
It is the shock of being forced out of the warm, dark liquid environment of the womb into cool air and light, noise and texture, that triggers your baby's first efforts to breathe for herself.

Huddling together to try and keep warm.
While contact between mother and newborn baby is better than none—

Marbles, rounders, twigs and [we found] string from the playground to do knitting.
Writing it into delivery-room rules or midwifery protocols is not a recipe for instant bonding—

Lovely, lovely, lovely to eat raw carrots.
And the more emphasis we place on it—

[Chuckles]
The more women feel that they have failed if that first meeting is delayed or they find themselves underwhelmed by it.

Swinging your arms, throwing your legs up into the air.
She cannot understand that there is a separate you.

The PT instructor was a wicked man. He used to push us in at the deep end.
Practising loving for her whole life.

Near misses.
She won't be able to control her behaviour in this first year.

Very brutal. We learnt to swim through fear.
The inappropriateness of punitive discipline in managing undesirable (or inconvenient and irritating) baby behaviour is no longer a matter of opinion but scientific fact.

Long stick and watch you floundering.
She cannot understand that you may want a 'minute to yourself.'

Senior girls made aprons. Undoing redoing undoing redoing.
Her brain that controls her social understanding and behaviour—the orbitofrontal cortex—only began to develop after she was born.

Because you didn't use the word beautiful. There was nothing beautiful about The Foundling.
You are rejecting a piece of language which was the best she had to offer.

I used to love cleaning shoes! Until this very day I just love it.
Modern technology has done nothing to lesson the sheer joy of books for babies.

If you had problems who could you talk to? Nobody.
Hers is a language of gestures, so precise that any interested person can understand them.

My mother never came once.
Mothers and newly delivered babies need time to be close and get to know each other, not only in the first hour after birth but in the first weeks. You will know when you have bonded with your baby because you will scarcely be able to distinguish his needs from your own, your main need being to meet his.

Maybe next time, maybe next time but next time never came.
Your newborn baby's bond with you is not a question.

Next time, oh she's bound to come!
We talk carelessly of 'independent life.'

Sunday bun. Dough cake. Bread pudding. A lump of raisins to eat.
A shopping expedition can be fun, but as long as shopping and bag are both safe for her, unpacking is the best part.

Wednesday night was called bashing up night.
How many signing and rhyming and tickling games do you know?
How many does she?

Throw carbolic soap at you. Stand on one leg with eyes closed, arms above our heads and they'd come round and hit us.
He is still physiologically dependent on your body to regulate his.

Frustrated, I believe. No outlet.
A tantrum is the explosive end result of a build up of tension, often frustration, usually with a mixture of fear and anxiety.

Just to get it out me system.
She may not only cry but scream and tremble, and she will not have the least understanding of a connection between anything she did and what you did.

You daren't tell tales.
It's rare for parents to be offered the time and space, the support and money they need, and many people will resent you taking it.

Captive 365 days a year.
He is even more likely to be clingy now than three months ago.

Don't forget it, you don't forget it.
Talk about anything that is making her interested, pleased or excited.

[Laughs]
Society will do little to help the two of you make room for your baby at the centre of your lives.

The war years were the blackest years.
Quarrels do not damage the love between you.

Life began to be wonderful.
The more she can love you—and other people to whom she is attached—and feel herself securely loved back, the more resilient, and generous in giving love she will be when she grows up—

[CHILDREN SINGING]
Once she can shout, your baby can sing.

[CHILDREN SINGING]
Babies have a powerful in-built drive for mastery that keeps them moving on.

The Healers

On the first day she lay food by my feet. Tupperware reused, tied in plastic bags, filled with lentils, aubergines, earth. Sat by my bed she read my hand, spoke of ladders, cogs & sky & moon. Holding a mirror up to my face she bade me, look. Days were shrouded in soil & shallow breath. She waited until I asked to be freed. Silver bangles like bells, she uncovered skin embittered with dirt, kissed my eyes. Out of her mouth crawled a child from a fairy tale who went underground. Separated black beans from white beans. Emerged with light shining between her fingers.

On the second day she arrived with bags of silence on her back, a bowl of olive oil in her palm, incense encircling like curls. She bade me, undress & lie down. Feathered hands obeyed as chest melted into clean towel. Fingers pressed on my back, deeper, deeper, until they went through me. I fell into an ancestral village, all my mothers' hands kneading wheat under the blaze of Indian sun. Lost body parts hid like buried jewels: earlobes, tops of ears, fingertips, insides of elbows, the ridge where neck meets hair. I found my voice under the bed, dusted & hung it under the sun.

On the third day holding my baby, she bade me, leave. Pack your books & run. She fed my baby apricots, plums & yoghurt, taught her to crawl, slept with eyes open. In the morning she drenched my baby's room in light, bathed her in coconut water, tickled her toes & when I returned, chest cavernous, having found each fingernail backs of knees elbows she draped me in a sari wound it around my body dressing a wound pressing silk into each pore of skin kissed my baby's feet & said *we are sisters healing we are healing souls sisters let me heal you sister healing we are sisters healing.*

VI. O

Saint Avia

after Saint Avia (The Jailed Woman)

CHAPTER 115

1. Raises her hand   fingers spread   at
their confessions.
2. Rich robes at mahogany desks.   Christ
hangs from the cross   watches plans get
nailed to paper   like her life.
3. Yet at each delivery of man   she raises
her hand   delivers a middle finger.
4. Fingers spread   she spreads her legs
fingers digging into sheets   deep
moans of women   deep in night
she might even cry *yes!*   Come.
5. Dawn of day   they force the key that
hangs heavy into the hole in the stone
walls.
6. A Bible snapping shut.
7. Her eyes turn to stone   her will hard
as rock bars of light thrown   between
bars of iron.
8. Woman at the window.
9. Spread across limestone floor   she
hears whispered prayers.
10. Head cocked to one side woman at
the window sees them on their knees
she pleads to Him   *please, make*
them fucking leave me be.
11. 'Kneaded by angels'   is the message
they spread   'delivered by light'.
12. But on knees   her lover's fingers
knead   rolling dough   soft like
skin   she presses fingers in   fingers
spread across the bread her lover
needs   fingers dig   hunger shape
of rocks waits by the window like
worshippers.
13. Or lovers or widows.
14. She swallows   as night cloaks all
watchful eyes   male & sinister
between hard rods of iron   they
spread their fingers   together
open-mouthed   full of bread & prayer
they whisper   eyes upturned   wet
oh God, oh God, oh God!

Open Mouths

I wanna go toilet. *Well that is not correct.* Unlike us language is not under lockdown.

How are you... today.

That first run was hard. My body feels like jelly. Like someone put their hand & arm inside me & rummaged around. Oh yes. That did actually happen.

We are sleeping. *She is sleeping better thanks.* Poo all over your jeans. Sweet scent of blondies in the living room air. I like looking at the rain from the inside. YOU AVERAGED 4 HOURS OF ACTIVITY ON YOUR PHONE A DAY LAST WEEK. Let's watch normal people fuck on tv while the baby sleeps. Touch quietly. Gasp in silence. *Shushhhhh* *Shushhhhh* YOU HAVE 568 NEW MESSAGES. Rolling belly. Soaking pained wrist. Cup of hot.

I'm sorry I can't be there for you. *Keep moving!* *If you can do it at home, do it at home!*

GET OFF THE GRASS MATE. *Get off your bike!* Totally ignored. Monkey Puzzle is a weird tree. I need to be alone.

In this aloneness.

Don't watch the news. Will you get sick of me?

Someone's someone's mum died. You send me a picture of you

wearing a mask. He can't have the job. He said, '*what was you sayin.*'

Who made the rules. Empty roads broke them. Empty pubs. Empty cafés.

Empty sounds. Stay. Away.

That wasn't two metres! Back up bitches! Sky stretches its arms.

Green is an open mouth.

A lone bird. I hear a piano instead of traffic.

What day is it. *Piano.* There's hair on the floor. Cba w cleanliness.

Rn. *Mmmmmm.* Profound morning chats between feeds. Another meme.

Bleach the world clean. & choke. It's a joke. To. Them.

We finally kiss again with open vowels.

Sorry you first. - *I thi-* *You go.* - *You froze-* *Say it again-* ... ?

Your Self-righteousness Pisses Me Off

& yet you are my friend, my cup of tea, my afternoon

so I cross into the kitchen, foot over sharp line

& yet you remain in another room

so we drink, burning tongues. I say, *fine*

& you say, *okay*. At the stairs

bitter leaves on teeth, you hug me

& your ear pushes my headphone into my ear

I say *ouch* while you tell me you love me

New Mouth

Kiki points at birds & bellows
words formed by her new mouth.
Her tongue flaps out
to show me her chewed

vowels that stretch to an 'o'.
Lips that kiss my lips.
Her made up sound doesn't sit
on the page but, like feathers, floats.

Do Not Open Your Mouths

I.

Daughters aren't allowed out at night but sons are.
bring shame onto families, hide it in their bellies.
cannot date.
cry at weddings, say goodbye. Marriage becomes a mourning.
are overripe mangoes, bright as turmeric inside.
do not swirl whisky in the ice cubes of their lives.
do not open their legs or get on their knees.
do not part lips.
wear pink.
hang up washing, roll rotis, douse themselves in oil.
should be tethered like feathers on a bird.
shouldn't pluck themselves loose.

2.

My daughter has Weetabix stuck to her chin.
has a sprig of brown hair sprouting from the top of her head.
blooms a bird chest.
is currently eating only beige foods, thank you very much.
loves *aminals*.
says, when you ask her age, *I 2 old*—and I agree.
mumbles *fucks sake*.
has a favourite word: *no*.
swats my hand away.
keeps busy pouring, mixing, building, climbing.
sings out of tune   & it rains.
stretches her arms   & it thunders.
is Midas, turns me into gold.
reaches for me, arms as mountains.
carries earth under her fingernails.
refuses to wash her hair.
refuses a kiss goodnight.
refuses to say goodbye.
on a swing is the moon pulling the tide.
rests her head on my chest as a prayer.
is a silent meditation.
shapes worlds, universes, galaxies, with her tiny hands, like God.

Anniversario

We order like pasta evangelists,
buy cheap wine from the corner shop,
tidy, lay mats, light a candlestick,
sit after six years, pause the clocks.
If we hadn't sat on a plane years ago
landed in salty air & gelato
unpacked our sadness, roamed Palermo
stone walls, fountains of shame & Mondello

where would we be swimming now. We clean sand
off her feet, which dots around the house
as miniscule reminders: our full hands
would be empty, other words would fill our mouths.
What is that we hear. It is the sea.
Waves blue & deep, breathing, like us in sleep.

Notes & Acknowledgements

'There Are No Birds' was commissioned by The Foundling Museum as part of the exhibition *Quentin Blake: Gifted.* Thank you to the editors Ella Frears and Sean Wai Keung for publishing 'A Feast of Phrases' in Magma magazine. 'The Healers' echoes a line from Roshni Goyate's poem 'Incantation (We are Healing our Sister)' from 4 BROWN GIRLS WHO WRITE (FEM Press, 2018). Thank you, Rosh, for letting me borrow this soulful verse. 'Teach Like A—' plays on language from the book *Teach Like a Champion* by Doug Lemov. 'Silent Night' echoes language from the poem 'XLV. – Because the Nile ran red with blood' – from *Asylum: A personal, historical, natural inquiry in 103 lyric sections* by Jill Bialosky (Knopf, 2020). 'Does Fire Ask Permission?' echoes lines from the poem 'Why I Left You' from *Violet* by Selima Hill (Bloodaxe, 1997). 'Saint Avia' is in conversation with the limestone sculpture 'Saint Avia' (The Jailed Woman), c.1450-1500, shown in *Reframed: The Woman in the Window,* Dulwich Picture Gallery, London. Caleb Femi's 'A Designer Talks of a Home / A Resident Talks of Home' from *Poor* (Penguin, 2020) influences 'The Found-Ling Poem.' 'Do Not Open Your Mouths' continues the conversation with one of my favourite poems, Caroline Bird's 'Little Children' from *The Air Years* (Carcanet, 2020). 'Anniversario' echoes lines from the poem 'It Is Here' by Harold Pinter.

Thank you, Pam, for letting me borrow your story, I hope I handled it with care. Thank you to Nina Pandora—'Wolf Mother' stemmed from one of our many strengthening conversations.

My deepest gratitude to Nina Hervé and Will Burns for believing in me when I didn't. Nina, you make the impossible possible. Will, you are the sharpest editor, pushing my writing in new directions. I can't thank you both enough for seeing the skies and mouths of these poems. Thank you to the wonderful Kate McQuaid for opening so many doors for me. Thank you to Craig Oldham and Eliza Hart for all your brilliant, thoughtful work on the cover, typesetting and my endless edits!

I am profoundly indebted to Roshni Goyate, Sheena Patel and Sunnah Qureshi Khan for 4 BROWN GIRLS WHO WRITE. We created something beautiful and I'll be forever grateful that we did it. Thank you to Rosh and Sheens for reading early drafts and giving me *compliments only please!* Thank you for the encouragement, advice and grounding friendship.

Thank you to my family: to Amrita Gill and Barbara Groves for your love and support, and especially to my parents, not only for your unwavering love and support, but for working hard all your lives so that I could do things like this.

Finally, for Kiran and Ravi, my sunbeams. And for Rory, for encouraging me to take that first poetry course, for being my first reader and for giving me something precious that newly born parents just don't have: time and space to write. You have given me everything good in my life. I dedicate this all to you.

Other titles by Sharan Hunjan

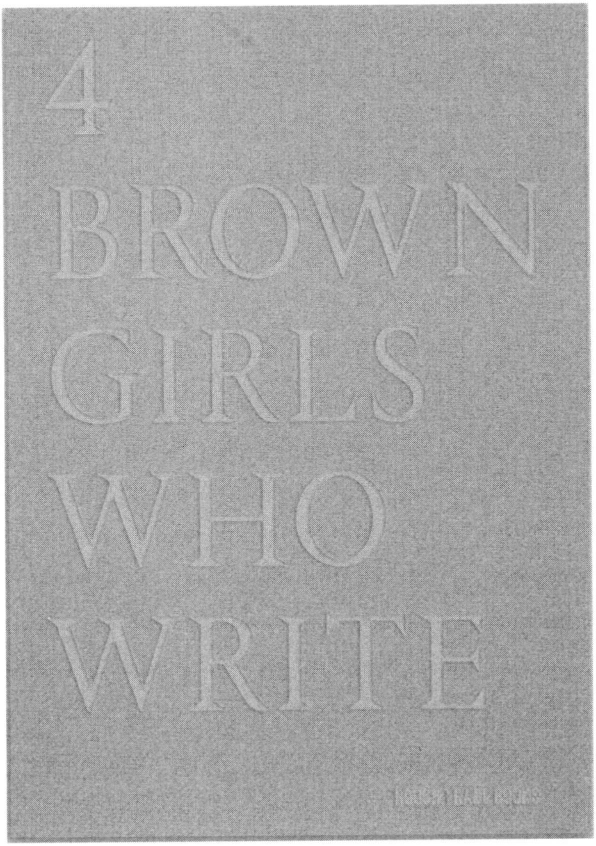

4 BROWN GIRLS WHO WRITE are Roshni Goyate, Sharan Hunjan, Sheena Patel and Sunnah Khan. These four writers that make up this talented collective bring their radical, polyphonic performance style to bear on a series of individual pamphlets that still resonate with their collaborative force. Each author's discreet publication is a stand-alone work, published here as a set of poetry and prose pamphlets, highlighting the daring, brilliant writing that characterises both the group and each individual author.

BUY HERE!

Rough Trade Books 2020

ROUGH TRADE BOOKS
roughtradebooks.com
9 781914 236402